Zelly, The Monster of Envy

The Monster Who Wanted It All

a WorryWoo tale

by Andi Green

Text and illustrations © 2015 Andi Green.
All rights reserved. No part of this book may be
reproduced without written permission from
the publisher, Monsters In My Head, LLC.

First Edition
Printed with Soy Ink

ISBN 978-0-9792860-6-3
Printed in China

For WorryWoo coloring pages, lesson plans
and more visit www.WorryWoos.com.

Zelly was an **envious** one,

so envious to the core...

Nothing was ever good enough—

he always **wanted more!**

He didn't like the things he had

and thought his friends had **better.**

He didn't like the clothes he wore—
his pants, his **shoes**, his **sweater.**

Zelly moped around with a

big 'ole frown—

he always looked so grim.

He thought that others had it all.

Why couldn't it be him?

His patience never lasted long;
his attention wasn't there.
Unless the **spotlight** was on **him**,
he really didn't care!

For a moment he was happy with
    the latest thing he owned,

but if something new should catch his eye,

he'd get jealous to the bone.

He often shouted "MINE! MINE! MINE!"

or yelled out "Give me that!"

Zelly's friends were growing tired of him
...acting like a brat!

At parties and on holidays,

Zelly always seemed so sad,

for he

needed,

wanted,

longed

to get what other

monsters had.

Spots of **green**
would then appear
each time he felt a twinge

of the
envy
that was
deep inside—
it was taking over him!

But a fateful day came Zelly's way
when he noticed in the sky,

a rainbow arcing through the clouds,
it shimmered way up high.

He held his breath then made a wish:

"I want to be a **king!**

Everything will be for **me:**

I won't share anything."

Zelly yaWNed
and stretched,
it was time to rest,
his eyes began to close…

And when he awoke he was in a room

with toys up to his nose!

There were presents

galore

upon the floor,
scattered everywhere,

Zelly walked around surprised to find

he now was in a **castle**,

with his portrait high upon a wall,

draped with a **golden** tassel.

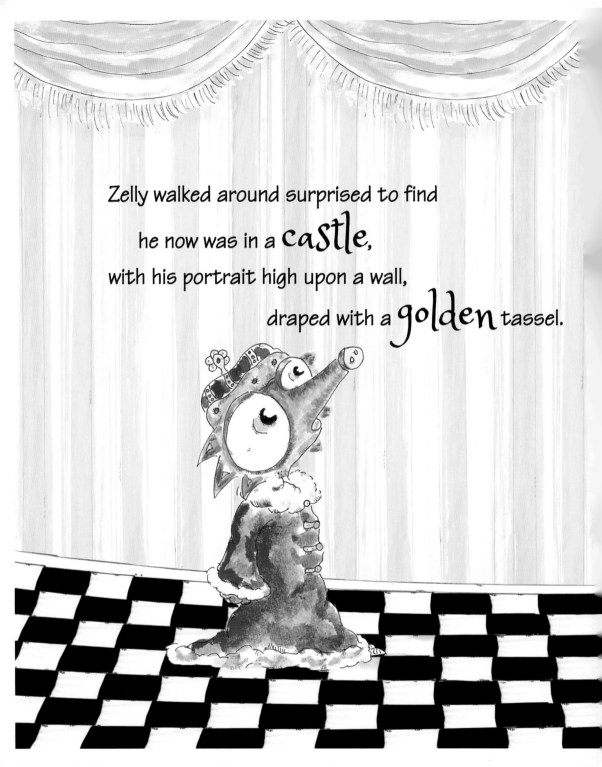

"*Your Majesty,*"
a voice then said,
"your" dinner
is prepared."

"Please do come down, and wear your
crown and sit in your grand chair."

"I am a **king**!"

Zelly sang with delight
as he danced around the hall.

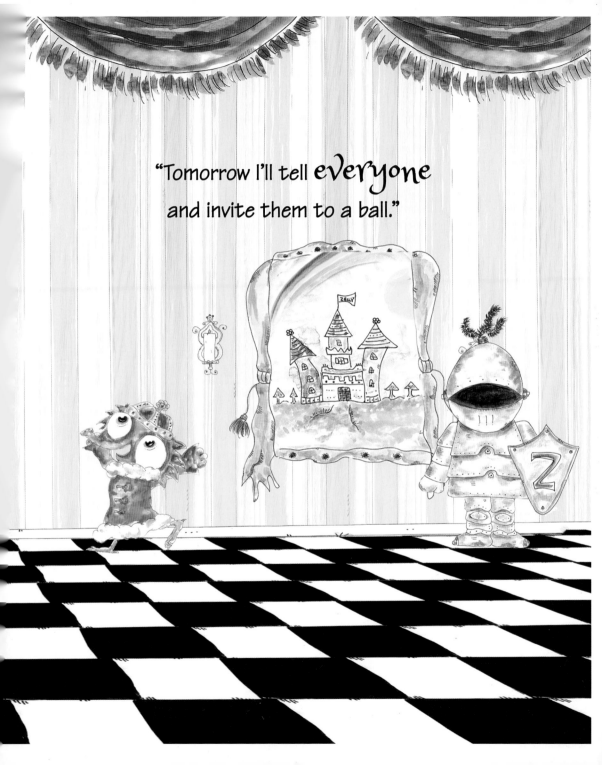

"Tomorrow I'll tell everyone
and invite them to a ball."

But Zelly soon forgot his plan,
his life was like a *dream...*

He lounged on squooshy pillows
and feasted on ice cream.

As days passed by, Zelly started to feel—
something
was amiss;

all the things that he had wished for
hadn't brought him
happiness.

Without someone there to share his fun,
Zelly finally came to see

that a **caStle** filled with lots of stuff
was **empty** as can be.

He thought of his friends and family
as he sat upon his throne;
was the wish he made
really worth the price of
being all alone?

Zelly grabbed his cape
and shiny **crown**
and to WooTown he departed.

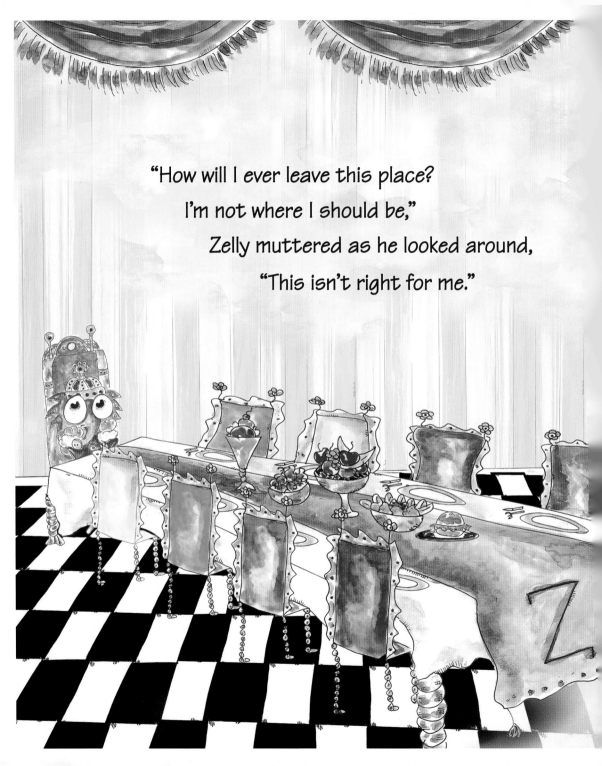

"How will I ever leave this place?
I'm not where I should be,"
Zelly muttered as he looked around,
"This isn't right for me."

"Your Majesty,"

a voice then asked,

"is there something wrong?

Perhaps you've begun to *appreciate*

what you once had all along?"

When he heard those words
Zelly understood exactly
what he'd done:
He had let his feelings
turn him **green**
by envying everyone.

He lost sight of what
had mattered most,
be it **big** or be it small—
for while he wanted this and that
...he already had it all.

Zelly yawned and stretched,
it was time to nap,
so sleepy was
the king,

and as he drifted off he said,
    "I **don't** need all these things."

Soon he was in a dreamy place,
remembering what had been.

The life that Zelly left behind

was *calling* out to him.

And in this
state of bliss
he heard

"Your dinner
is prepared."

Zelly opened up his eyes to see—

his family standing there!

Surrounded by the ones he loved

Zelly **NOW** had everything!

...how it felt to be a king.

The End

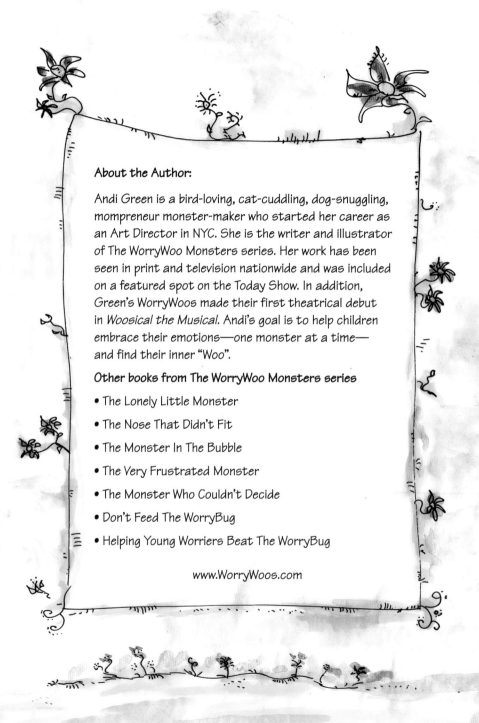

About the Author:

Andi Green is a bird-loving, cat-cuddling, dog-snuggling, mompreneur monster-maker who started her career as an Art Director in NYC. She is the writer and illustrator of The WorryWoo Monsters series. Her work has been seen in print and television nationwide and was included on a featured spot on the Today Show. In addition, Green's WorryWoos made their first theatrical debut in *Woosical the Musical*. Andi's goal is to help children embrace their emotions—one monster at a time—and find their inner "Woo".

Other books from The WorryWoo Monsters series

- The Lonely Little Monster

- The Nose That Didn't Fit

- The Monster In The Bubble

- The Very Frustrated Monster

- The Monster Who Couldn't Decide

- Don't Feed The WorryBug

- Helping Young Worriers Beat The WorryBug

www.WorryWoos.com